Best Wishes
Reginald John Finlay

June 13, 1987

# THE
# COMPLETE
# BOOK OF
# WALL STREET ETHICS

**SPURIOUS BOOKS IN THIS SERIES**

*Connoisseurs' Guide to the Wines of South Dakota*
*The New York Transit Authority Book of Customer Service*
*The Vatican Guide to Family Planning*
*Nude Beaches of British Columbia*
*Readers' Guide to the Novels of Jorge Luis Borges*

# THE
# COMPLETE
# BOOK OF
# WALL
# STREET
# ETHICS

## JAY L. WALKER

**WILLIAM MORROW AND COMPANY, INC.**
*New York*

Library of Congress Catalog Card Number: 87-60125

ISBN: 0-688-07393-X

Printed in the United States of America

First Edition

1 2 3 4 5 6 7 8 9 10

BOOK DESIGN BY RICHARD ORIOLO

**"You can be greedy and still feel good about yourself."**

**—IVAN BOESKY**